The Red Beast Anger Workbook

by the same authors

The Red Beast
Helping Children on the Autism Spectrum to Cope with Angry Feelings
K.I. Al-Ghani
Illustrated by Haitham Al-Ghani
ISBN 978 1 83997 275 1
eISBN 978 1 83997 276 8

Winston Wallaby Can't Stop Bouncing
What to do about hyperactivity in children
including those with ADHD, SPD and ASD
K.I. Al-Ghani and Joy Beaney
Illustrated by Haitham Al-Ghani
ISBN 978 1 78592 403 3
eISBN 978 1 78450 761 9

Are You Feeling Cold, Yuki?
A Story to Help Build Interoception and Internal Body Awareness for Children
with Special Needs, including those with ASD, PDA, SPD, ADHD and DCD
K.I. Al-Ghani
Illustrated by Haitham Al-Ghani
ISBN 978 1 78775 692 2
eISBN 978 1 78775 691 5

The Panicosaurus
Managing Anxiety in Children Including Those with Asperger Syndrome
K.I. Al-Ghani
Illustrated by Haitham Al-Ghani
ISBN 978 1 84905 356 3
eISBN 978 0 85700 706 3

Making it a Success
Practical Strategies and Worksheets for Teaching
Students with Autism Spectrum Disorder
Sue Larkey
ISBN 978 1 84310 204 5

Practical Sensory Programmes
For Students with Autism Spectrum Disorder and Other Special Needs
Sue Larkey
ISBN 978 1 84310 479 7
eISBN 978 1 84642 567 7

The Red Beast Anger Workbook

*For All Children Who Want to Tame Their Red Beast
Including Those on the Autism Spectrum*

K.I. Al-Ghani
and **Sue Larkey**

Illustrated by Haitham Al-Ghani

Jessica Kingsley Publishers
London and Philadelphia

First published in Great Britain in 2023 by Jessica Kingsley Publishers
An imprint of John Murray Press

1

A CIP catalogue record for this title is available from the
British Library and the Library of Congress

ISBN 978 1 83997 415 1
eISBN 978 1 83997 416 8

Printed and Bound in Great Britain by Bell & Bain Limited

Jessica Kingsley Publishers' policy is to use papers that are natural,
renewable and recyclable products and made from wood grown in
sustainable forests. The logging and manufacturing processes are expected
to conform to the environmental regulations of the country of origin.

Jessica Kingsley Publishers
Carmelite House,
50 Victoria Embankment,
London, EC4Y 0DZ, UK

www.jkp.com

John Murray Press
Part of Hodder & Stoughton Limited
An Hachette UK Company

Contents

Introduction for Adults   7

1. Meet Danni and His Family   11

2. Danni Learns Ways to Calm the Red Beast   17

3. The 14-Day Challenge   21

4. What Wakes Up a Red Beast?   25

5. What Does Anger Feel Like in the Body?   31

6. What Wakes Your Red Beast?   35

7. Time to Take Stock   39

8. The Power of Words   43

9. Time to Train the Brain to Use Kind Words   53

10. A Negative Attitude   63

11. Perfectionism   69

12. Winning and Losing   77

13. Sensory Things   91

   USEFUL TOOLS AND OTHER IDEAS   109

Introduction for Adults

Emotional flooding is an outpouring of fear and anxiety that can lead to anger, aggression or total shutdown if we don't understand how to deal with it.

It is often termed a "meltdown" but is really **an involuntary coping mechanism.**

The words **"involuntary"** and **"coping"** will be crucial to our understanding of how to respond to them.

The term "meltdown" refers to the process of melting metal.

It helps to think of a meltdown, quite literally, as a melting pan. The contents have boiled dry and everything that was once solid begins to lose shape and takes on a new and now dangerous form. Can we turn off the heat before that molten metal overflows and causes more damage or harm? Can we become more vigilant and prevent it from happening so frequently?

Imagine a child with special needs being overwhelmed by sensory overload, by the constraints and demands of others and by their own expectations. Powerful emotions will bubble up and spill out as fear and anger. This is the experience of emotional flooding and safely supporting a meltdown can be frightening and always difficult. Yet, as adults, we realize that it is our responsibility to recognize them, understand them and try to become a safe container for these uncontrollable emotions.

It is not just the child who needs coping strategies but the parents, grandparents, brothers, sisters, aunties, uncles, cousins, teachers, support assistants and anyone who cares for or works with children who simply cannot yet self-regulate their powerful feelings.

What is happening in the brain, during a meltdown, is critical to our understanding of it. It is termed the "amygdala hijack" and happens when we react to psychological stress as if it is physical danger.

The amygdala is one of two almond-shaped structures of nuclei, found deep in the temporal lobe of the brain. Among other functions, it is responsible for the fight-or-flight mechanism. If the amygdala senses danger, it will suddenly trigger an intense, unconscious, emotional response, that effectively switches off the thinking brain (the neocortex). Once activated, there are only five things we can do, known as the five Fs: fight, flight, freeze, fluster, flock (see What Wakes Up a Red Beast?).

What happens next is a cascade of visceral responses, starting with the release of adrenaline, leading to increased heart rate, blood pressure and breathing, followed by shaking, sweating and possible nausea or stomach problems.

Stress hormones, like cortisol, make it almost impossible to concentrate or problem solve.

The toll it takes on the child is significant and it may take several hours before any sense of equilibrium is restored.

> **The amygdala has everything to do with protection and not connection. We cannot extinguish these emotional fires by talking.**

Children who develop better impulse control will do better at school and at life in general.

Most children with special educational needs have problems linked to executive function (the mental processes that help us to plan, focus attention, remember instructions and juggle multiple tasks) and they are more likely to be delayed in reaching emotional maturity.

If we want to learn how to switch off the amygdala, we need to train the brain to use a default mechanism that needs to be stored in our long-term memory. Only then will we be able to access it automatically, without too much thought.

> Getting these strategies into long-term memory takes compassion, patience and, above all, practice.

This workbook is aimed at doing just that.

It isn't going to be a quick fix – it will be a formative and illuminating journey towards understanding and self-control.

While you can be too young to embark on this journey (the brain can't do what it hasn't yet developed), you can never be too old.

We invite you to join Danni as he starts his journey towards understanding and regulating his anger.

How to use this book

To ensure the child's journey is well paced, we have included breaks at appropriate points. At these points, you can hand the child one of the "take a break" cards that can be cut from the back of the book or downloaded from www.jkp.com/catalogue/book/9781839974151.

Most of the written activities can be completed within the book, or downloaded from www.jkp.com/catalogue/book/9781839974151, printed out, and filled in separately. Likewise, all of the colouring pages are downloadable.

The quick recap quiz later in the book can be done verbally and recorded or written down, or – depending on the child – it could form part of a summative assessment. You could even tell the child that it is a quiz to see how well you have been helping them. You may have to explain some of the words in the quiz.

There are several picture-based discussion prompts included at the back of the book to help reinforce what the child is learning.

Chapter 1

Meet Danni and His Family

Hi,

My name is Danni.

I love all electronics, walking my dog, Dolores, and going fishing.

When I am busy doing the things I enjoy, life is just perfect.

However, sometimes life can be tough.

You see, I can get very angry – very, very quickly.

It takes everyone, including me, by surprise.

My dad says anger seems to be my default, so I am working hard on trying to change it.

This is my grandma; I sometimes go to her when I am feeling sad.

Grandma says we all get angry from time to time because we can't choose our feelings, but we can choose what to do about them.

She says it is okay to be angry, but it's not okay to:

◊ hurt people
◊ say mean things
◊ destroy property.

It makes me feel very bad when I do any of these things, so I am going to work really hard to try to control my actions.

This is my teacher, Mr Parker.

I really like and respect him.

He says everyone gets angry from time to time, but when I get angry, it is like a switch flips on really quickly.

Mr Parker says I need to try to change that flip switch to a dimmer switch.

If I can do that, he says it will give me time to try to get control of my anger and make some better choices.

This is my Uncle Charlie; he takes me fishing.

I love fishing and it is always a good time to talk about things because I feel relaxed.

My uncle says being angry can make us all lose control and before we know it, we could be in danger. He knows, because he used to get angry too, when he was my age.

He showed me that putting a "D" for "Danni" in front of the word "ANGER" spells "DANGER".

He says anger can make us be in danger of doing something stupid or hurting ourselves or someone else. We might lose control and do or say something we later regret and feel really sorry about.

Uncle Charlie says anger is in all of us and it's our job, as we get older, to try to learn ways to handle it better.

This is my mum. She is a writer and she loves horse riding. I can always depend on Mum to help me to calm down.

Mum says anger is inside all of us, like a Red Beast. Most of the time it is asleep, but sometimes it wakes up.

She says it is very important to learn how to calm that beast so it can go back to sleep.

Discussion: What do you think about Danni?

ACTIVITY I: COLOUR IN THE PICTURE OF THIS SLEEPY RED BEAST

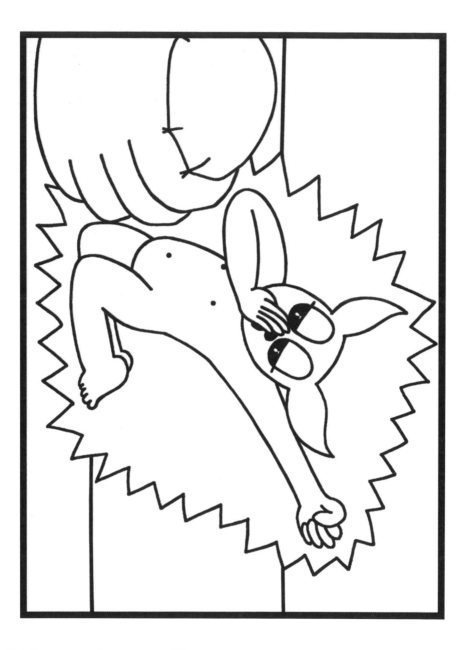

Time to: Take a Break Card

The Red Beast Workbook

Chapter 2

Danni Learns Ways to Calm the Red Beast

My family and my teachers are helping me to find ways to try to calm my Red Beast.

In this workbook, I am going to show you what helps me the most.

I asked my family what they did to make their Red Beast go back to sleep.

This chart shows some of the things my family and I do to keep calm.

When angry, it helps to:	Activity	Danni	Grandma	Dad	Mum	Uncle Charlie
	Breathe and count slowly from 1 to 20	✔	✔	✔	✔	✔
	Go for a run	✔				✔
	Do some fun exercises to music		✔		✔	
	Read a book, comic, paper, Happy Scrap Book (see Useful Tools and Other Ideas)	✔	✔	✔	✔	
	Do some arts and crafts	✔	✔	✔	✔	
	Have a drink and snack		✔	✔	✔	✔
	Play computer games/ construction games/puzzles	✔				✔
	Stroke a pet	✔	✔	✔	✔	✔
	Watch TV or YouTube videos	✔	✔	✔	✔	✔

ACTIVITY 2: ....'S KEEP CALM TABLE

When angry, it helps to:	Activity	Me	A friend	My teacher/ TA/helper	Family member	Family member
	Breathe and count slowly from 1 to 20					
	Go for a run					
	Do some fun exercises to music					
	Read a book comic, paper, Happy Scrap Book					
	Do some arts and crafts					
	Have a drink and a snack					
	Play computer games / construction games/puzzles					
	Stroke a pet					
	Watch TV or YouTube videos					

Danni Learns Ways to Calm the Red Beast

Here are some more things to try to calm the Red Beast.

When angry, it helps to:	Activity	Me	A friend	My teacher/ TA/helper	Family member	Family member
	Listen to music					
	Sleep under a heavy blanket					
	Watch the night sky					
	Smell your favourite things like vanilla/ chocolate/mint/lemon					
	Paint a picture					
	Drink hot chocolate					
	Squeeze a toy					
	Roast marshmallows					
	Go to a special place, like a tent, tree house, library, bedroom					
	Dig in the garden					

Discussion: Can you think of something to add to these calming activities?

Time to: Take a Break Card

The Red Beast Workbook

Chapter 3

The 14-Day Challenge

Learn How to Tame Your Red Beast Just Like Danni

I was set a 14-day challenge to practise things that would help me to put the Red Beast to sleep – I had to do this mindfully, when I was in a good mood.

This is my chart showing some of the things I did each day for the challenge – at school and at home.

I was awarded a certificate after I finished doing the calming things for 14 days.

Danni's Home/School 14-Day Challenge Chart

School day/date	I used my Red Beast Box* to practise calming the Beast. These are some things I tried:	Draw ☺
Day 1 *School* 1/2/22	Used the stress ball and counted down from 20 to 1, then… Burst some bubble wrap, had a drink, read a comic	☺
Day 2 *School* 2/2/22	Used the stress ball and counted down from 20 to 1… Watched the liquid timer, had a drink, did some construction	☺
Day 3 *School* 3/2/22	Used the stress ball and counted down from 20 to 1… Listened to some music, had a drink and ate some grapes	☺
Day 4 *School* 4/2/22	Used the stress ball and counted down from 20 to 1… Burst some bubble wrap, had a drink, did ten minutes on my tablet	☺
Day 5 *School* 5/2/22	Used the stress ball and counted down from 20 to 1… Coloured a picture of the Red Beast, had a drink with straw, did ten star jumps	☺
Day 6 *Home* 6/2/22	Used the stress ball and counted down from 20 to 1… Baked cookies, drank milk, stroked Dolores	☺
Day 7 *Home* 7/2/22	Used the stress ball and counted down from 20 to 1… Went in the pop up tent, read a comic using a torch, had some cereal	☺
Day 8 *School* 8/2/22	Used the stress ball and counted down from 20 to 1… Burst some bubble wrap, watched the liquid timer, had a drink and a protein bar	☺
Day 9 *School* 9/2/22	Used the stress ball and counted down from 20 to 1…	
Day 10 *School* 10/2/22	Used the stress ball and counted down from 20 to 1…	
Day 11 *School* 11/2/22	Used the stress ball and counted down from 20 to 1…	
Day 12 *School* 12/2/22	Used the stress ball and counted down from 20 to 1…	
Day 13 *Home* 13/2/22	Used the stress ball and counted down from 20 to 1…	
Day 14 *Home* 14/2/22	Used the stress ball and counted down from 20 to 1…	

*See the Red Beast Box at the end of the book.

The Red Beast Workbook

You can fill in your own challenge chart here or download a copy.

Add to it each day – at home and at school.

. . . .'s Home/School 14-Day Challenge Chart

School/ home/ date	I used my Red Beast Box to practise calming the Beast. These are some things I tried:	Draw ☺
Day 1	Used the stress ball and counted down from 20 to 1, then…	
Day 2	Used the stress ball and counted down from 20 to 1, then…	
Day 3	Used the stress ball and counted down from 20 to 1, then…	
Day 4	Used the stress ball and counted down from 20 to 1, then…	
Day 5	Used the stress ball and counted down from 20 to 1, then…	
Day 6	Used the stress ball and counted down from 20 to 1, then…	
Day 7	Used the stress ball and counted down from 20 to 1, then…	
Day 8	Used the stress ball and counted down from 20 to 1, then…	
Day 9	Used the stress ball and counted down from 20 to 1, then…	
Day 10	Used the stress ball and counted down from 20 to 1, then…	
Day 11	Used the stress ball and counted down from 20 to 1, then…	
Day 12	Used the stress ball and counted down from 20 to 1, then…	
Day 13	Used the stress ball and counted down from 20 to 1, then…	
Day 14	Used the stress ball and counted down from 20 to 1, then…	
You did it!	Download your certificate:	

ACTIVITY 3: SLEUTH PUZZLE

Find all the words that mean "happy".

a	j	o	y	f	u	l	h	f	u	o	p	a	c
o	v	e	r	j	o	y	e	d	o	e	d	g	o
l	g	p	i	o	p	l	e	a	s	e	d	e	n
e	u	y	d	e	l	i	g	h	t	e	d	e	t
l	u	f	s	s	i	l	b	a	l	b	l	t	e
l	d	l	r	e	x	u	l	t	a	n	t	o	n
y	y	t	u	e	j	e	e	e	u	p	a	a	t
d	l	r	h	x	e	t	j	o	k	i	n	g	e
o	a	l	r	j	c	h	p	c	j	d	t	e	d
t	h	l	o	e	t	p	c	l	a	i	v	o	j
p	i	y	g	j	m	j	u	b	i	l	a	n	t
p	e	a	c	e	f	u	l	u	f	e	e	l	g
f	y	r	e	c	s	t	a	t	i	c	j	l	p
u	e	l	d	h	a	p	p	y	a	s	e	o	c

Ecstatic
Joking
Joyful
Cheerful
Peaceful
Elated
Exultant
Merry
Jovial
Pleased
Jubilant
Overjoyed
Happy
Contented
Delighted
Glad
Gleeful
Blissful
Jolly

(Answers are at the end of the book.)

Further activity: Can you put these "happy" words in order of intensity?

Time to: Take a Break Card

Chapter 4

What Wakes Up a Red Beast?

Once I knew how to calm the Red Beast and put him back to sleep, I needed to figure out what woke him up.

My Uncle Charlie says these are things called **triggers**.

He says that deep inside everyone's brain is a place called the amygdala (pronounced: am-ig-duh-luh).

A trigger can set off a reaction in the amygdala – the part of the brain that senses trouble.

(Actually, there are two of them, one on each side of the brain.)

Amygdala

Amygdala

Uncle Charlie says that brains are made to do this to keep us aware of danger, so we can stay safe.

The amygdala is part of our most primitive brain and develops first – it is sometimes called the "reptilian brain".

If we feel anxious or afraid (which I do, quite a lot of the time), the amygdala switches on automatically and when this happens, the thinking brain gets switched off.

My uncle says that if the amygdala has learned to be over-protective, it may press the panic button too soon and then all we can really do when this happens is one of five things – called the five Fs.

These are: FREEZE, FLEE, FIGHT, FLUSTER and FLOCK.

1. FREEZE

Freeze is when you totally shut down.

Imagine someone getting a real shock and then fainting – this is the freeze mechanism.

2. FLEE

Flee is the urge to run away and hide.

I know this feeling!

3. FIGHT

Fight is really what I do – I get angry and aggressive. I don't mean to – it just happens because the job of my amygdala is to protect me from harm. My uncle told me that the amygdala starts off a chain reaction that causes blood to flow to my heart and muscles. Then the body is flooded by some things called hormones, like adrenalin (that make my body strong and powerful), and this gives me the energy to run or fight. It also affects all my insides, so I sometimes feel sick or queasy, get stomach cramps or urgently need the toilet.

4. FLUSTER

Fluster is when we can't think straight – like forgetting our lines in a play (stage fright), not knowing how to answer exam questions (panic) or like my mum when she failed her driving test for the third time.

My uncle told me that when fluster sets in, the stress hormone – called cortisol – makes us feel shaky, sweaty and sick and our thinking brain gets switched off, so we can't read anything, our mouth gets dry, so we can't speak and we can't listen to what people are saying.

5. FLOCK

Flock is when we go to a place or a person where we can feel safe.

At home, it is Mum and Grandma, and at school, it is Mr Parker.

Uncle Charlie said I should try to train my brain to FLOCK instead of FIGHT or FLEE.

All the things I practised in the 14-day challenge will help to switch off my amygdala and switch my thinking brain back on.

My grandma reminded me that when I was little, I didn't need to think what to do when I got upset because somebody was always there to help me. When you are very young, somebody usually comes to the rescue and helps you feel better – but as we get older, folks expect us to help ourselves.

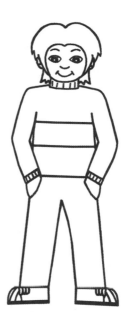

Grandma says it isn't easy if we have an over-protective brain – but it is possible, with patience and plenty of practice.

ACTIVITY 4: CAN YOU LABEL THE Fs AND GIVE EXAMPLES OF WHAT MAY CAUSE THEM?

F........	
F........	
F........	
F........	
F........	

Discussion: How does your amygdala react when it is being over-protective?

Time to: Take a Break Card

The Red Beast Workbook

Chapter 5

What Does Anger Feel Like in the Body?

After I learned what helped me to calm my Red Beast, it was time to take notice of how my body felt when I was angry.

When I am angry:

I can feel my heart beating	I start to shake
I feel hot	I feel sweaty
I start to shout	I scowl at people
I say mean things	I stamp my feet
I feel a knot in my stomach	I hit out
I make fists with my hands	I throw things
I break things	I feel out of control
My mouth feels dry	I start to cry

Discussion: Can you add to this list (e.g. point your finger, roll your eyes, get bossy, feel jealous)?

ACTIVITY 5: CAN YOU LABEL THE PLACES ON THE BODY THAT ANGER CAN BE FELT (E.G. HEART BEATING FAST, KNEES SHAKING)?

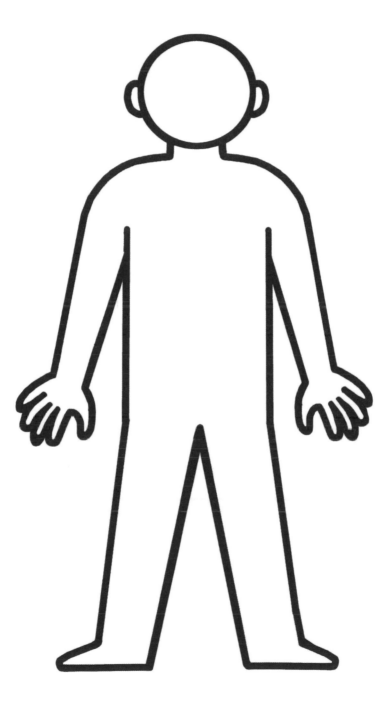

ACTIVITY 6: COLOUR THIS PICTURE OF A VERY ANGRY RED BEAST

Time to: Take a Break Card

The Red Beast Workbook

Chapter 6

What Wakes Your Red Beast?

ACTIVITY 7: WHAT WAKES YOUR RED BEAST?

Tick or draw an angry face next to what wakes your Red Beast.

Does this wake your Red Beast?	Tick or draw an angry face ✔ 😠
1. Having to wait	
2. Losing a game	
3. Being touched or bumped into	
4. Being scared	
5. Thinking people are making fun of me	
6. Thinking something is unfair	
7. Doing tests	
8. Being late	
9. Being tired	
10. Being ignored	
11. Loud noises	
12. Being left out	
13. Being bullied	
14. Things not going as planned	
15. Not understanding what to do	
16. Being told what to do	
17. Technology not working	
18. Being hungry	
19.	
20.	

Can you add to the list?

The Red Beast Workbook

ACTIVITY 8: COLOUR IN THIS PICTURE OF A FIGHTING RED BEAST

ACTIVITY 9: SLEUTH PUZZLE

Find all the words that mean "angry".

r	r	e	t	t	i	b	o	i	d	i	v	i	l
i	p	e	e	v	e	d	n	s	a	f	h	i	y
t	d	o	v	d	r	f	c	u	a	l	d	d	l
m	g	e	t	m	l	e	r	o	i	f	e	e	u
t	a	s	h	a	d	d	n	i	e	v	u	y	f
a	i	d	m	n	f	t	e	r	o	i	q	o	e
n	d	e	c	r	e	i	f	u	a	q	i	n	t
g	d	g	n	i	m	u	f	f	e	g	p	n	a
r	g	m	d	h	e	a	t	e	d	m	e	a	h
y	r	f	h	t	s	s	o	r	c	n	r	d	a
n	u	e	d	g	i	r	r	i	t	a	t	e	d
u	m	i	i	n	f	u	r	i	a	t	e	d
f	p	a	i	o	d	e	d	n	e	f	f	o	y
s	y	e	t	i	t	d	e	x	e	v	a	e	a

Enraged
Angry
Inflamed
Peeved
Bitter
Heated
Irritated
Mad
Grumpy
Cross
Hateful
Livid
Fuming
Vexed
Annoyed
Offended
Fierce
Infuriated
Piqued
Furious

(Answers are at the end of the book.)

Further activity: Can you put these "angry" words in order of intensity?

Time to: Take a Break Card

Chapter 7

Time to Take Stock

Before moving on, let's review what we have learned so far and see how much you have remembered by doing this quick quiz.

ACTIVITY 10: QUICK QUIZ   SCORE . . . . /25

Date . . . .

Name . . . .

1. What does Danni's uncle say about anger and Danni's name?

   Daft   Danger   Dippy   Dotty

2. What is the name of Danni's dog?

   Dotty   Dylan   Dolores

3. What is the name of Danni's teacher?

   Mr Parker   Mr Peters   Mr Pollard

4. What did Danni's mum say anger looked like?

   A red balloon   A red baboon   A red beast

5. Tick all the things that Danni tried to control his anger.

   Drink and snack   Breathe and count

   Stroke a pet   Play computer   Read a comic

6. List four things that help you feel calm.

   a . . . .

   b . . . .

   c . . . .

   d . . . .

7. The amygdala in the brain switches on when we feel afraid or anxious.

   True   /   False

8. How many days did Danni practise calming his Red Beast for the challenge?

   7   14   10

9. Anger is in all of us.

   True   /   False

10. How are you doing controlling the Red Beast?

   Still trying   Getting better   Much better

Finished — thank you.

Time to: Take a Break Card

Chapter 8

The Power of Words

Doing this workbook has made me think about things I do when I get angry that upset others.

I sometimes say horrible things to people.

I don't mean to and I am always sorry afterwards.

I want to try to stop myself doing this.

My grandma told me that words can hurt or heal.

I found this difficult to understand, so she took me into the kitchen to explain!

Grandma helped me to understand what she meant about words hurting or healing.

We needed a sieve, some icing sugar and some baking beans.

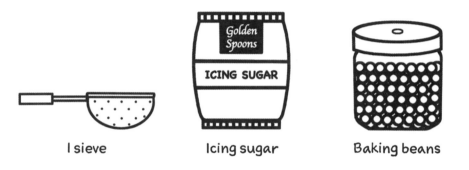

| I sieve | Icing sugar | Baking beans |

Grandma explained that a sieve helps us to filter things, like flour or icing sugar. Our brain is a bit like a sieve – it helps us to filter our thoughts.

She said to think of the icing sugar as kind, gentle, nice, thoughtful or sweet words – we can use these words without thinking too much, because everyone loves a kind word.

The baking beans are like hard, mean, unkind and thoughtless words – we should try to keep these from spilling out of our mouths because they can really hurt people's feelings and that can make them feel bad or sad or mad.

Grandma said we must think about the power of words because cruel words can harm or hurt people.

Discussion: Can you think of a time someone hurt your feelings with mean words?

Grandma said sweet words are like giving someone:

A present

A box of chocolates

A piece of cake

An ice cream sundae

A firework display

A cute kitten

Discussion: What other things would people like as a gift?

Grandma told me that saying horrible, mean, unkind, cruel or thoughtless words can hurt people – they are like giving them:

A really bad smell

A loud noise that hurts the ears

A sore toe – ouch!

Horrible tasting medicine

Discussion: Can you think of some more horrible things that people wouldn't like to get?

Time to: Take a Break Card

Grandma said there are lots of horrible words that people use when they get angry.

There are **threatening words**.

She told me that some people might use threatening words to tell others that they are going to hurt them or hurt someone or something they love and care about.

Threats make people feel afraid.

These are words like:

I'm gonna get you!

Just you wait and see what I am going to do to you!

Discussion: What must it be like for someone who is being threatened at school or at home?

Then, Grandma mentioned **insulting words**.

Insulting words are when people say something to someone that makes that person feel bad about themselves:

Words like:

    stupid

        idiot

            ugly

                fat

                    useless

                        selfish.

Discussion: Have you heard anyone use insulting words?

Grandma told me there are **cruel words**.

Cruel words can make people feel sad, lonely and unloved.

Words like:

    I hate you!

        Get lost!

            You're not my friend!

                You are such a loser!

                    Leave me alone!

Discussion: Can you think of some cruel words you may have heard?

Of course, we all know, there are **swear words**:

Grandma said that people hear lots of swear words on television, in chat rooms, on YouTube and in some grown-up films.

Kids may use them to shock, to sound older or to get attention.

Grandma told me that swear words should never be used in school or on the school playground – either by children or adults.

Sometimes, when people accidently hurt themselves or feel very disappointed, swear words may jump right out of their mouth before they can be stopped.

Grandma said we should try to think up different words to say when we feel disappointed or if we accidently hurt ourselves.

We could use **funny words** like: Sugar! Bother! Fudge! Shoot!

Cheese and crackers! Smelly socks!

Grandma said the problem with swear words is that they can just jump out of the mouth, even when we don't want them to.

She told me that using them a lot makes them more jumpy, but using them less means they won't be so jumpy.

When people are angry, it is easy to say hurtful words – they just spill out.

Grandma said as soon as anyone knows they have said some horrible things, they should say, "I didn't mean to say that, I'm sorry."

ACTIVITY 11: CAN YOU THINK OF SOME BETTER WORDS TO SAY INSTEAD OF SWEAR WORDS?

Make a poster of these better words for home and the classroom.

Time to: Take a Break Card

The Red Beast Workbook

Chapter 9

Time to Train the Brain to Use Kind Words

Grandma said that training ourselves to use kind words will help us to filter our thoughts (remember the sieve?) and think before we say anything we might later regret.

Sweet words can be kind, pleasant, polite, gentle, thoughtful or funny.

Grandma told me a great way to use kind words is by giving people a compliment. Compliments are thoughtful words that tell people what we like about them and they make people feel special.

Grandma told me that a great way to remember what compliment words are is to think TAPS:

Things
Appearance
Personality
Success

You could TAP someone on the shoulder to give them a compliment.

Grandma and I made a table to show how to use compliments.

TAPS	COMPLIMENTS
Things:	I really love your new trainers!
	Your new bike is awesome!
	Is that a new lunchbox? It's great!
	Your dog is so cute!
Appearance:	Your hair looks great!
	I like the way you wear your cap.
	That colour really suits you.
	Your fancy dress costume looks amazing.
Personality:	You always make me feel happy.
	You are a great listener.
	I wish more people were like you.
	Your passion always amazes me.
	I'm glad I am on your team.
Success:	You should be proud of yourself.
	Wow! You really did well on that test.
	My mum says you are very polite.
	Your hard work really shows.

Discussion: Have you ever given or been given a compliment?

Time to: Take a Break Card

Grandma still had more to say on the power of words.

She said that some words become kind when we say them with warmth and a smile:

Thank you.

Come in.

Oh, great to see you.

I am so glad you came.

I love it when you come to visit.

ACTIVITY 12: PLAY THE GAME: WHAT DID I SAY? WHAT DID I MEAN?

Instructions:

1. Paste the Phrases and Tone of Voice sheets onto cardboard and cut into strips along the dotted lines.

2. Make one pile for phrases and another for tone of voice.

3. Each player picks a phrase and a tone of voice.

4. That person leaves the room with you and you make a video of them saying the word using the tone of voice chosen.

5. When all the cards have been used, play back the video and see who is the quickest to recognize the tone of voice.

What Did I Say? What Did I Mean?
Phrases
Stick on card, cut into strips along the dotted lines and laminate.

1. Come in

....

2. So glad you came

....

3. Sit down

....

4. Great to see you

....

5. Take a seat

....

6. Your hair looks great

....

7. Is that a new school bag?

....

8. Do you want a drink?

....

The Red Beast Workbook

What Did I Say? What Did I Mean?
Tone of Voice
Stick on card, cut into strips along the dotted lines and laminate.

1. Say the phrase using a gentle tone of voice

....

2. Say the phrase using an angry tone of voice

....

3. Say the phrase using a sad tone of voice

....

4. Say the phrase using a bored tone of voice

....

5. Say the phrase using an impatient tone of voice

....

6. Say the phrase using a suspicious tone of voice

....

7. Say the phrase using a sarcastic tone of voice

....

8. Say the phrase using a funny tone of voice

....

Grandma said that some words are
sweet because they show we care:

Do you need help?
Can I help you?
Hey, let me do that for you.
Don't worry, I will do that.
Let me get the door for you.

Would you like me to do anything for you?
Let me carry that heavy box.
You go, I will tidy up.
Shall I make some tea?

Grandma told me that when we use sweet words they make us feel good inside.

This is because when we use them, people will know we are a nice person and, guess what...they will treat us nicely too.

It's cool to be kind!

Discussion: Words are powerful — what will your words do today?

Time to: Take a Break Card

Chapter 10

A Negative Attitude

Another thing that upsets others is something my family mentioned to me. They tell me I sometimes have a negative attitude.

My mum told me that the only thing that can hold you back in life is having a negative attitude.

I didn't really understand what she meant.

Mum told me that if you do one or all of the following things, you may have a negative attitude to life:

1. Shouting

Well, I definitely do shout – a lot – especially when I am angry.

2. Pouting

I sometimes pout when I can't get my way or if I don't win at a game.

3. Clouting

Yup, anger makes me hit out sometimes – that's clouting!

Mum said it was time for another challenge.

She said ATTITUDE is a little thing that makes a BIG difference to how people see you.

We can either have a positive and good attitude or we can have a negative and bad attitude.

Uncle Charlie said he had to learn the hard way that with a bad attitude he could never have a good day – but with a good attitude he never had a bad day.

Attitude is the way you mentally look at the world.

Uncle Charlie told me if you can't change your fate – that is, what happens in your life – then try changing your attitude.

My uncle said the attitude and the choices people make today will be their life tomorrow. When you make the choice to be pleasant and positive – that is how others will treat you.

He said a positive or good attitude is like a magnet for getting positive and good results.

ACTIVITY 13: THE FOUR-WEEK CHALLENGE: BECOME A MORE POSITIVE PERSON

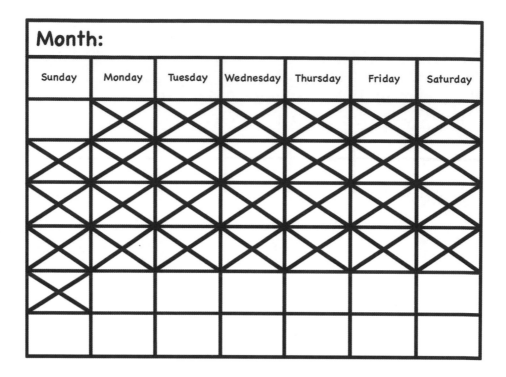

Month:						
Sunday	Monday	Tuesday	Wednesday	Thursday	Friday	Saturday

Change your bad attitudes for good ones for just four weeks. This will programme your brain and you and others will see a new, more positive you.

Month:						
Sunday	Monday	Tuesday	Wednesday	Thursday	Friday	Saturday

I chose to try this challenge in the school holidays when I would be more relaxed.

I got a certificate when I completed it.

Join me because attitude is everything and positive things happen to positive people.

Discussion: When will you try the four-week attitude challenge and get your certificate?

Time to: Take a Break Card

Chapter 11

Perfectionism

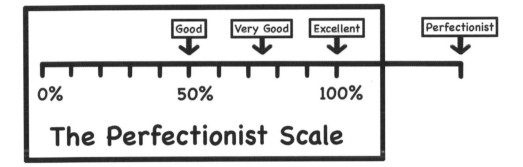

Something else that makes me angry is when things aren't perfect.

If I make a mistake I feel really stressed.

This usually ends up with me shouting and destroying things.

I think if I make a mistake people will see me as stupid.

Thinking this way makes trying new things scary for me.

I just feel so frustrated and angry as I can't see another way to make things right.

Mum said that it is nice to get things right or have high standards, but everyone makes mistakes.

This is just part of being human – we all make mistakes.

My grandma said I am a bit of a perfectionist.

She told me that it is good to push ourselves to do our best, but it is not good to get angry and upset if we make mistakes.

Grandma said making mistakes is just part of learning.

Mistakes are proof that we are trying.

When we get something wrong, we must not forget about all the things we did right.

Mistakes have the power to turn us into something better than we were before.

Trying to achieve perfection, she says, will only make us feel bad about ourselves. We will become anxious and, as you know, anxiety switches off our thinking brain.

Grandma said being anxious about making mistakes gets in our way. It steals away confidence and happiness.

Mum said that sometimes things in life just don't work out perfectly.

Usually we can't do much about them, but we should always have a back-up plan – just in case things go wrong.

She reminded me of the time we went swimming and the place was closed due to technical problems.

I really lost it and had a big meltdown in the car.

Since then, if we go anywhere I am excited about, we always make a Plan B – just in case things go wrong.

Instead of swimming, we might go bowling or to the adventure playground.

If we go to the supermarket and they don't have exactly what I want, I always have a Plan B list of other stuff, just in case.

My Uncle Charlie thought this was a brilliant idea and he reminded me that there are 26 letters in the alphabet, so we could have Plan B right through to Plan Z – I think he was just joking!

My Uncle Charlie made a poster for me to put on my bedroom wall:

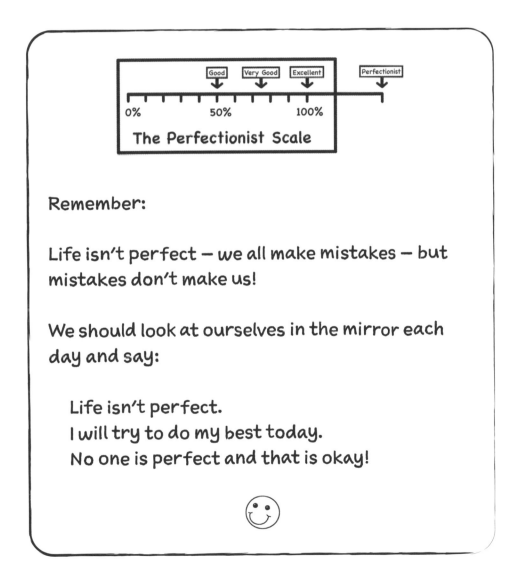

Remember:

Life isn't perfect – we all make mistakes – but mistakes don't make us!

We should look at ourselves in the mirror each day and say:

Life isn't perfect.
I will try to do my best today.
No one is perfect and that is okay!

ACTIVITY 14: DANNI'S DIFFICULTIES WITH PERFECTIONISM

Discussion: Can you help Danni to find any more solutions to his problems?

Oops – the problem	Can we fix it?
Angry – because his pencil lead broke so he snapped the pencil in half.	Sharpen the pencil. Always keep extra sharpened pencils in a see-through pencil case. Use a propelling or twist-up pencil.
Mad at losing a small piece of LEGO® – so broke it up.	Join the LEGO® club to get missing pieces for free.
Angry – threw his sandwich in the bin because Mum didn't cut it how he liked.	Learn to make your own sandwiches and cut them using a chopping board, clean ruler and sharp knife.
Sad and angry – after missing a goal during football, stormed off the pitch.	Count backwards from 7 to 1. Take some deep breaths. Later – watch videos of your favourite players missing goals and see what they do. Make a plan of what you will do if you miss a goal, and practise it before a big game.

ACTIVITY 15: START KEEPING A LIST OF YOUR OWN PERFECTIONIST PROBLEMS – AS THEY TURN UP – BOTH AT HOME AND AT SCHOOL

You could even take photographs.

Ask an adult if you need help to make your list.

Oops – the problem	Can I fix it?

Chapter 12

Winning and Losing

My teacher, Mr Parker, reminded me of something that can make most people, even grown-ups, get angry.

Losing at a game.

I don't know why, but it just makes me see red.

I can't stop the mean words coming out, and later, when I have had time to cool down, I often feel bad about what I said and did.

My teacher thought it would be a good thing for all the class to think about this.

This is what he told us...

One thing most people, of all ages, like to do is play games.

We play all sorts of games – team games, computer games, as well as board games.

The goal to playing a game is to try to win.

Winning is fun, and it can make us feel happy, proud and special.

Usually, only one person or one team can be the outright winner.

Won   Lost

When we play games there will be times when we win and times when we lose.

Won   Runner up

Mr Parker said losing isn't fun, but we can still feel good if we try our best, follow the rules and accept losing with courage and dignity – this is called being a good sport.

Mr Parker explained that courage and dignity mean congratulating the winners, not blaming or being mad at ourselves or our teammates for making mistakes.

He said it takes courage and dignity to keep our emotions calm.

To help to stay calm and dignified we can:

1. Breathe in and count slowly backwards from 7 to 1.

2. Think about something else, like how many planets we can name, or how many dinosaurs we know.

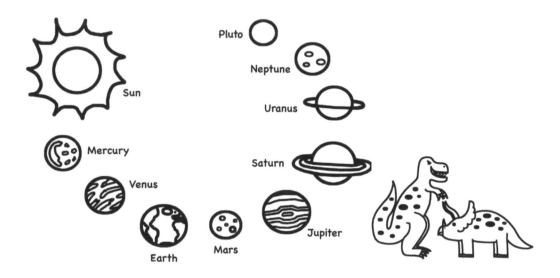

(This is called an anchor thought and it helps to switch off the amygdala.)

3. Literally "Pull yourself together" by sitting down, taking a deep breath, arms crossing the chest, holding the upper arms and then pulling down into the chair or into the ground as you slowly breathe out. This shows courage and dignity.

4. Take a break and go to get a drink with a straw and a snack.

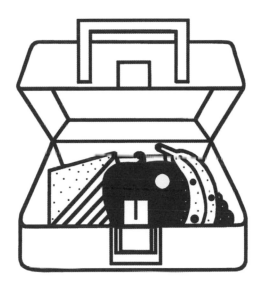

Mr Parker told us we can still be winners to ourselves, our friends, teachers and families, if we accept losing with courage and dignity, as this will help us to control our anger.

Good sports show dignity and good manners when they lose, for example:

◇ saying "Congratulations", "Good job", "Great game" to their teammates or opponent
◇ shaking hands
◇ smiling and walking calmly away.

Mr Parker also said that some winners can spoil the winning moment by:

◇ doing extreme fist pumps and celebrating.
  It is okay to say "yes!" – but one time only.
  It is okay to fist pump – but one time only.
  It is okay to be happy – but stay calm and dignified
    – don't over-do it.
◇ saying things like: "WE WON! YOU LOST!" or calling the other team or person "LOSERS!"
◇ bragging* – a good sport leaves it to others to say how brilliant they are and accepts it calmly as a compliment.

(*Bragging means to say how wonderful you are – other ways of saying this are: to boast, to swank, to swagger, to sing your own praises, to blow your own trumpet, to fly your own kite! – not something a good sport should do.)

Some people who lose can spoil the moment or the game by losing badly – for example by:

◇ pouting

◇ being angry at the winner

◇ name calling

◇ complaining that it isn't fair!

Mr Parker says all players should try to be good sports.

By being a good sport, we may have lost the game, but he says we will always win the respect and friendship of the other players and the spectators.

Not everyone loves a winner, but everyone loves a good sport.

Being a Good Sport makes you a Great Player

Our teacher showed us some videos so we could see examples of people losing badly and losing with courage and dignity – it was certainly an eye-opener!

Mr Parker made some "good sport" cards to give the class when we lost a game with courage and dignity and this meant we got extra time to enjoy free choice activities.

I'm a Good Sport

_____
Name

_____   _____
Date   Sign

Discussion: What do you think about those famous sports people who have got angry during a televised event?

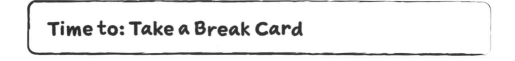

Time to: Take a Break Card

ACTIVITY 16: COLOUR THIS PICTURE OF DANNI CALMING HIMSELF

Chapter 13

Sensory Things

The Eight Sensory Systems

Sound   Sight   Smell   Taste

Touch   Proprioceptive   Vestibular   Interoception

Quite often, I just don't feel right and I don't know why and this sometimes makes me angry.

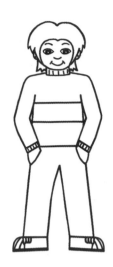

I find it hard to know if I am hungry, thirsty, too hot, too cold, not feeling well, or if I feel happy or safe.

It means I worry a lot.

I have something called sensory processing disorder (SPD).

Our brains get messages from all our senses, but, for me, these messages can be difficult to read and understand.

Our bodies and brains have to do so many things at the same time and when everything works well, we have something called HOMEOSTASIS (o-mee-o-stay-sis). When we have this, we enjoy some feel-good things, like being happy, comfortable and contented.

If we don't have homeostasis, then we feel out of sorts and this makes me feel angry with myself and everyone else.

Discussion: Do you have any sensory issues?

A person called an occupational therapist (OT) helped me to understand about my body and my senses.

This is what I have learned:

You probably know all about our five senses. These are:

Sound   Sight   Smell   Touch   Taste

I bet you didn't know we have some more.

These are:

Proprioception
This is about movement.
The brain gets messages from muscles and joints.

Vestibular
This is our sense of balance controlled by the inner ear – it tells my body if I am upside down, or going backwards.

Interoception
This is what we are feeling inside – hungry, thirsty, tired, ill, angry, happy and so on.

The Eight Sensory Systems

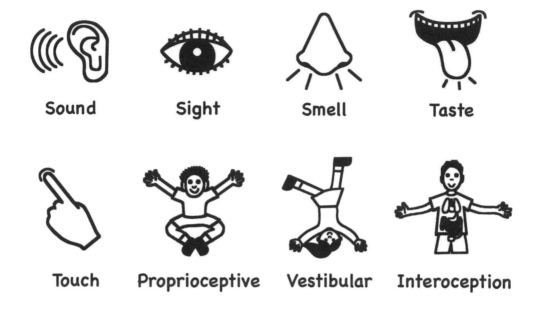

Sound   Sight   Smell   Taste

Touch   Proprioceptive   Vestibular   Interoception

Yup! No kidding – eight sensory systems!

My OT told me we can think of the sensory system as having a different bowl for each of these eight senses.

These bowls need to be just the right size, so everything is well organized and feels right. If you have SPD your bowls may not be the right size.

If we are over-sensitive to the sense of touch, then that bowl is too small and too much input will cause it to overflow and we may find things touching us very annoying or painful, e.g. wearing socks, labels in clothes, or someone brushing past us.

If we are under-sensitive to the sense of touch then that bowl is much too big – so we may enjoy really big bear hugs or being wrapped up tight in a blanket or wearing a weighted jacket, and we may not be very sensitive to pain.

In a body where the sensory inputs are working properly, the bowl is always just right and so everything is working well.

Each sense has its own bowl, so you can be over-sensitive to one sense and under-sensitive to another.

I don't like certain smells, noisy places or things like vacuum cleaners and hand dryers. I don't like bright lights or going out in the sunshine and I can get angry when people just brush against me. I also chew my collars and cuffs.

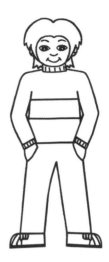

So, my bowls for smell, sight, touch, sound and taste are too small.

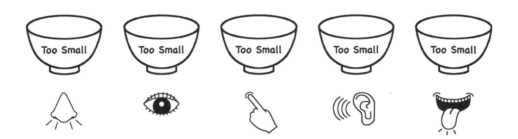

On the other hand, my proprioceptive and vestibular bowls are very big. I love hanging upside down and spinning round and I never get dizzy and I am always running, jumping and dancing.

My sense of interoception is also affected by SPD.

This sense is very important because it tells my brain to tell my body to take action, if I am too hot, too cold, too thirsty, too hungry, too tired, not well and so on. It should let me know how I am feeling inside – but my brain doesn't seem to understand the messages and I just don't feel good, but I don't know why.

This can relate to my feeling angry – if I am too hungry I don't always know this, but I start to feel bad and it can make me get angry. Mum says I am not angry, I am "hangry" and I need to eat something – and you know my mum is always right!

What size are your sensory bowls?

The Red Beast Workbook

Danni's bowls

Too big? Under-sensitive	Which sense?	Too small? Over-sensitive	Which sense?
Too Big I can't get enough – give me more, more, more!		It's too much – take it away! I feel overwhelmed!	
I am under-sensitive to:		**I am over-sensitive to:**	
Trampolining Swinging Running and jumping		Vacuum cleaners Lawn mowers Yelling/shouting Fire alarms	
Spinning around Hanging upside down Rocking on my chair		Labels in clothes Seams in socks People brushing past me/crowds/lining up at school	
I don't know...when my body feels hungry or thirsty, if I am too hot or too cold, I am sick, I am tired		Strong sunlight Flickering lights Strip lights Glare on windows	
I like to chew my collars and cuffs		Cooking smells (especially school canteen) Petrol fumes Newly washed clothes Perfumes and hairspray	

ACTIVITY 17: WHAT ARE YOUR SENSORY BOWLS LIKE?

Too big? Under-sensitive	Which sense?	Too small? Over-sensitive	Which sense?
Too Big I can't get enough – give me more, more, more!		Too Small It's too much – take it away! I feel overwhelmed!	
I am under-sensitive to: Make a list:		I am over-sensitive to: Make a list:	

Sound   Sight   Smell   Touch   Taste

Proprioception   Vestibular   Interoception

Once I learned all about my sensory issues, it was time to see if I could figure out how to help myself, so I wouldn't feel grumpy or out of sorts.

Problem? Over-sensitive	Can I fix it?
(eye)	Wear a cap with a visor. Wear tinted glasses. Stay in the shade. Put down window blinds.
(ear)	Wear ear defenders when out in busy or noisy places – like the playground – but only for short periods of time. Wear headphones and listen to soothing music when working. Ask the school to alert you when there will be a fire drill. Record sounds you don't like and play them back for short periods to try to get accustomed to them.
(nose)	Wear wristbands impregnated with your favourite smell. Keep a clean handkerchief or mask that you can put over your nose.
(hand)	Let friends and family know you are sensitive to light touch. Ask the teacher if you can go ahead of the line or be placed at the back. Cut out labels from clothes, wear seamless socks.
(mouth)	Instead of chewing collars and cuffs, it would be better to use a chew stick or chew jewellery (see Useful Tools and Other Ideas for a list of sensory tools).

Problem? Under-sensitive	Can I fix it?
I am under-sensitive to: Proprioception	This means I need more input for my muscles and joints. I can't get enough information – so I am very fidgety. **At home, I can:** • jump on my trampoline • go on my swing • go for a run • go under a heavy blanket • get a big bear hug. **At school, I can:** • have regular movement breaks • sit on a wiggle cushion • have an anti-rock chair • wear a padded vest or shoulder toy for short periods.
Vestibular	This means my brain needs to get more input to keep my sense of balance. **At home, I can:** • sit upside down in my favourite chair • dance around, especially spinning • climb the tree in my garden • pace up and down in the garden. **At school, I can:** • stand at a high table or bench to do my work • take sensory breaks to do cartwheels and handstands in the playground • sit on a wobble cushion or exercise ball • do sensory circuits before school starts.

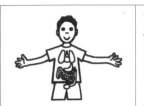 Interoception	This means I don't always know how I am feeling inside — I just don't feel good, but I don't know why. If I am hungry or thirsty, I may get angry. At home and at school I need to practise being mindful.* **At home, I can:** • keep a check on when to eat and drink • check my body temperature if I don't feel good, to know if I am sick • have a regular sleep pattern. **At school, I can:** • take frequent snack and water breaks • take regular toilet breaks.

*Being mindful is keeping an awareness of thoughts, feelings, body sensations and the environment, through a gentle nurturing lens — like meditation and yoga.

ACTIVITY 18: SEE IF YOU CAN FIGURE OUT HOW YOU CAN HELP YOURSELF WITH SENSORY UNDER- OR OVER-SENSITIVITY

Problem? Over-sensitive	Can I fix it?
	This means I may not like strong sunlight or flashing lights.
	This means I may not like sudden or loud noises.
	This means I may not like certain smells.
	This means I may not like certain foods or drinks.

	This means I may not like someone touching me, wearing socks or the labels in clothes.
	This means I may not like too much exercise, like running and jumping.
	This means I may not like swings, seesaws or a merry-go-round.

Problem? Under-sensitive	Can I fix it?
	This means I may like flashing lights, lava lamps and being out in the sun.
	This means I may enjoy loud music and I may talk too loudly.
	This means I may like to smell things like shoes or leather chairs.
	This means I may like sucking lemons and having lots of salt on my food.
	This means I may like big bear hugs, weighted blankets and waistcoats.
	This means I may not know when to stop eating or drinking.

	This means I may need more input for my muscles and joints. I can't get enough information, so I may be very fidgety.
	At home, I can:
	At school, I can:
	This means my brain needs to get more input to keep my sense of balance:
	At home, I can:
	At school, I can:
	This means I don't always know how I am feeling inside – I just don't feel good, but I don't know why. If I am hungry or thirsty, I may get angry.
	I need to practise being mindful both at home and at school.
	At home, I can:
	At school, I can:

Time to: Take a Break Card

The Red Beast Workbook

Useful Tools and Other Ideas

TAKE A BREAK: 1
A relaxation break

I could:

- count backwards from 7 to 1
- do deep breathing
- listen to soothing music
- go to my imaginary world for 15 minutes.

TAKE A BREAK: 2
A sensory break

I could:

- chew gum/chewy tube
- watch a liquid timer
- sit in a pop-up tent
- wear a weighted vest/ blanket.

TAKE A BREAK: 3
A solitude break

I could:

- go to my room
- go to the safe haven
- read a book/comic
- read my Happy Scrap Book.*

* See Useful Tools and Other Ideas.

TAKE A BREAK: 4
A diversion break

I could:

- do a job – gardening, cooking
- do construction toys
- go to see a friend/relative/ teacher
- use electronics for 10/15/30 minutes.

The Red Beast Workbook

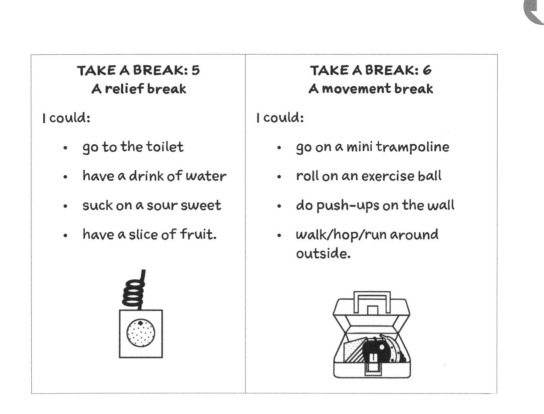

TAKE A BREAK: 5
A relief break

I could:

- go to the toilet
- have a drink of water
- suck on a sour sweet
- have a slice of fruit.

TAKE A BREAK: 6
A movement break

I could:

- go on a mini trampoline
- roll on an exercise ball
- do push-ups on the wall
- walk/hop/run around outside.

You can either cut out these cards or download a copy from www.jkp.com/catalogue/book/9781839974151

The Red Beast Box

Danni found the Red Beast Box a great tool to use when he was trying to calm his Red Beast.

Get an adult to help you put together your own Red Beast Box.

It could include:

- ◇ stress ball
- ◇ eye masks
- ◇ bubble wrap
- ◇ relaxation music
- ◇ scented pillow – for example, lavender, vanilla, chocolate
- ◇ a bottle with a straw for water
- ◇ foods to replenish blood sugar – for example, dates, grapes, raisins, nuts
- ◇ sensory toys – see sensory supports.

Discussion pictures from
The Red Beast book

Discussion: Can you think of something that may wake a Red Beast in the picture? For example: the couple having a picnic — perhaps a wasp flies in.

Discussion:

1. What happened to Danni?
2. Was he hurt?
3. What other things may have made Danni get angry?

Discussion:

1. Why did it help Danni to go to the special room to calm down?
2. What things helped him?
3. What things help you?

The Red Beast Workbook

Discussion:

1. Why was the teacher pleased with Danni?
2. Do you think your class would like a reward jar?
3. What things might the class do when the jar
   is full?

Discussion:

1. How do you think Danni felt when he saw Charlie in the classroom?
2. Have you ever apologized to anyone — what did you say?

The Red Beast Workbook

The Happy Scrap Book

Science tells us our mood changes when we see images of things that we love.

Looking at images you love when you are feeling sad, anxious or angry will make you feel better.

Make a Happy Scrap Book with photos or samples of your favourite things, for example:

- ◊ pastimes
- ◊ interests
- ◊ hobbies
- ◊ books
- ◊ comics
- ◊ DVDs
- ◊ TV/YouTube
- ◊ colours
- ◊ smells
- ◊ textures
- ◊ pets/animals
- ◊ people
- ◊ foods
- ◊ places
- ◊ toys.

Or whatever makes you smile...

Certificates

These can all be downloaded in colour.

The Red Beast Workbook

Suggested reading

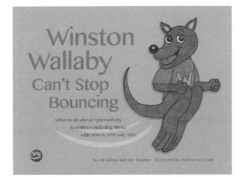

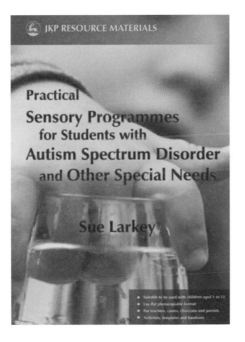

Sensory tools

For sensory tools visit: https://suelarkey.com.au/sensory-shop.

This Red Beast Thermometer is downloadable.

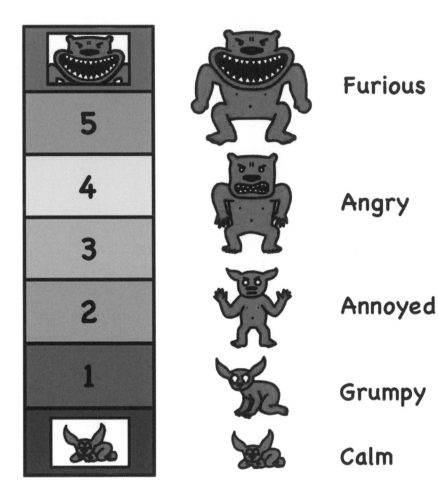

The Red Beast Workbook

Ideas for using The Red Beast Thermometer in the classroom

This vertical thermometer uses words and colour to describe the stages of the Red Beast on a five-point scale. Here are some ideas for using the thermometer:

1. Children could use a thesaurus to brainstorm words for the various stages.
2. Children could create a Red Beast "menu" describing what makes their Red Beast develop from calm to furious – here are some ideas:
   ◊ **Calm:** Doing my special interest/horse riding/trampoline/computer/music/massage.
   ◊ **Grumpy:** Being told I must leave my special interest and do something else/getting up in the morning/people touching my stuff.
   ◊ **Annoyed:** A change of plan from a favoured activity to something else without warning, for example computer crashing, swimming pool out of use, teacher absence.
   ◊ **Angry:** People making fun of me/doing handwriting/school assemblies.
   ◊ **Furious:** People trying to talk to me when I am angry/loud voices and angry faces of other people/broken equipment/lost equipment/being forced to do something I feel afraid of, such as tests.
3. Use a cut-out of a favourite character to stick on the scale to show how they are feeling.

More able children could write or tape stories of how they tamed the Red Beast.

Answers to the sleuth puzzles

Activity 3: Happy

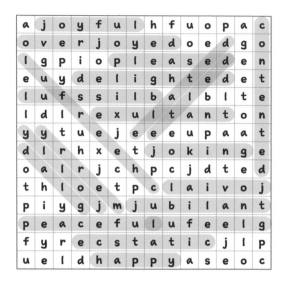

Activity 9: Angry

The Red Beast Workbook